Thistle Hill

The History and the House

THISTLE HILL

The History and the House

By Judy Alter

Foreword by Lloyd "Cissy" Stewart   Illustrations by Barbara Whitehead

Texas Christian University Press
Fort Worth

Library of Congress Cataloging-in-Publication Data

Alter, Judith MacBain, 1938–
Thistle Hill: the history and the house.

1. Thistle Hill (Fort Worth, Tex.) 2. Architecture,
Georgian—Texas—Fort Worth. 3. Architecture, Domestic
—Texas—Fort Worth. 4. Wharton family. 5. Scott family.
6. Fort Worth (Tex.)—Biography. 7. Fort Worth (Tex.)—
Buildings, structures, etc. I. Whitehead, Barbara.
II. Title.
F394.F7A48   1988   976.4'5315   87-10251
ISBN 0-87565-074-0 (pbk.)

Designed by Whitehead & Whitehead

This book is printed on acid-free materials

Contents

THISTLE HILL
is listed in the
National Register for Historic Places
and is a
Recorded Texas Historical Landmark.

Acknowledgments

MANY THANKS are due Keith Gregory, who conceived the idea for this book when he was director of the TCU Press, and Deborah Phelan, former executive director of Texas Heritage, Inc., who spent many hours supplying information and reading the manuscript.

x

The front steps, with oversize stone flowerpots, possibly reflecting Mrs. Scott's interest in the gardens and flowers.

Foreword

THISTLE HILL is Fort Worth's castle. Like the castles peppered throughout Europe, it remains as tangible evidence of another age. Texas cattle barons who built such castle-like homes ruled more territory than most of those European noblemen who lived in castles, but their subjects were cattle, not people, and they held power for a far shorter time. The era of the cattle baron began in the 1880s and had disappeared by the 1920s. The great Texas ranches were established by men who fought their way through Indian raids, the Civil War and Reconstruction, trail drives, droughts and financial panics to a legendary "Cibola" of wealth. Ironically, that wealth, lavished on their children, destroyed many of their sons and daughters.

If a man had a large, successful ranch in the northern part of Texas, he felt he owed it to his family to build them a lavish home in Fort Worth. A whole row of these mansions survived until World War II, but Thistle Hill stood out among them. Any child who grew up in Fort Worth fifty years ago learned to identify Thistle Hill by its water tower—which most of us believed was a watch tower to spot marauding Indians. We could only glimpse the mansion itself—and imagine what went on in the house behind those high brick walls.

When I returned to Fort Worth in 1949 as a reporter for the *Fort Worth Star-Telegram*, the Girls Service League was operating the Scott Home, as it was known then, as a residence for working girls. It was a needed service at that time, when young women often worked at jobs paying twenty dollars a week or less.

I received my basic education on Fort Worth people

and their personal history from two remarkable women, Mary Sears Rhodes, who was women's editor of the *Star-Telegram*, and Pauline Naylor, who was federated clubs editor. Pauline Naylor always said she worked at the *Star-Telegram* instead of playing bridge. It was one of her hobbies; another was collecting fine china, silver and linens while her husband, John W. Naylor, collected rare books. I was a guest in their home one evening when conversation turned to the Scott Home. Pauline Naylor brought out a dozen dessert plates, each decorated with a different bird "after Audobon," and dozens of lace-trimmed white napkins. All of them had been wedding gifts to Georgia Scott Townsend. Winfield Scott's only daughter, who had lived in the mansion off and on, sold her possessions for money to live on late in life.

Fort Worth is a relatively young city. Only in recent years has it realized the importance of preserving its landmarks and recording its history. In the 1970s, I wrote about the drive to "Save the Scott" and assigned Sandra Hawk—now Mrs. Tony Record—to write one of the first stories crediting the Girls Service League with its part in the preservation of the mansion. But like almost everyone else, my knowledge of Thistle Hill and the families who lived there was part legend, part fantasy, and part fact.

The lifestyle of Texas cattle barons, represented by Thistle Hill, already has become mixed with legend. Tourists often mix historical Fort Worth with television "Dallas." But Thistle Hill proves by its very existence a way of life which helped form Fort Worth and the State of Texas. Judy Alter has recorded not only the history of the architecture but also that of the families who lived in the mansion and the story of its preservation, so future generations can visit and wonder and dream about Fort Worth's castle.

Lloyd "Cissy" Stewart
Fort Worth
September 1987

xii

Thistle Hill ~ The History

The Cattle Baron Legacy

THISTLE HILL, a three-story Georgian Revival style mansion, sits on a slight natural rise in the landscape of the hospital district, close to Fort Worth's downtown area. Its large, double city-lot site is surrounded by concrete and steel—buildings taller than the house itself—and paved streets. When built in 1903, Thistle Hill stood alone on its small hill, dominating the scene around and commanding attention from the residents of the surrounding wealthy neighborhood, then known as Quality Hill. It sat on Pennsylvania Avenue at the foot of Summit, then known as Hill Avenue.

Today, Thistle Hill survives as visible evidence of a way of life now long gone, a way of life closely tied to the cattle kingdoms of North Central Texas. It symbolizes the way Texans used their energies, land and material resources to develop vast personal fortunes and to contribute to the growth of Texas and the Southwest. The cattle barons, as they were known, were people whose lives had been touched by all the major stories of the Old West—cattle drives, Indian raids, the Civil War, even gunfights—but many of them survived those dangers and hardships to enter the twentieth century with wealth and a style in many ways unequalled since.

The cattle barons were also civic builders. The cities they lived in grew in population, business, and wealth, and cattle money contributed to the building of great churches, railroad stations, courthouses and other public buildings. Without the cattle baron lifestyle,

The leaded glass front door, with an arched fanlight which repeats the semicircular motif found throughout the house.

brought alive today in this elegant home, Fort Worth would be neither the metropolitan center it is today nor the historic reminder of the cattle kingdom.

Thistle Hill has had only two private owners, the A. B. Whartons, Jr., and the Winfield Scotts. Tradition has it that the house was built in 1903 by cattleman W. T. Waggoner for his only daughter, the beautiful Electra, as a wedding present. When Electra married Philadelphian Albert B. Wharton, Jr., Waggoner sought a way to ensure that his daughter would remain in Texas rather than moving east. This honeymoon cottage was his way of securing her in Texas, or so the story goes. Actually, the house may well have been initially planned by the newlyweds before they left for an extended honeymoon in Europe, but construction was not announced until after their return. The bride's father may have been a consultant, but he did not build the house singlehandedly. The best architects in Fort Worth, the firm of Sanguinet and Staats, were hired to design the house in the Colonial Revival style. One suspects that the orders to the architects were to spare no expense. Construction began in 1903 and is said to have cost approximately $38,000. The house has eighteen rooms, six baths, and slightly over 11,000 square feet.

By 1900, the city of Fort Worth had grown beyond its rough frontier origins. It had survived the post-Civil War depression and the Panic of 1883 and had seen the railroad arrive, followed by packing plants which seemed to ensure the city's future as a meat-packing center. Following the prediction of newspaperman B. B. Paddock, who foresaw that refinement would necessarily follow wealth, the city had grown into a community of fine homes with tree-shaded sidewalks and an elegant, even luxurious lifestyle for those whose wealth was based on the cattle grazing on ranges to the north and west of the city.

The Whartons moved into their new home in 1904, almost two years after their wedding. Already they were the parents of one son, Tom Waggoner Wharton. A second son, Albert B. Wharton III (Buster), was born in 1909 during their residence in the mansion. In 1910 when Waggoner distributed his ranching empire among his three children, giving each land, cattle and

The limestone pillars of the front porch, taken from the west.

horses valued at about 2 million dollars, Electra and Albert put Thistle Hill up for sale and moved to their ranch property near Vernon, Texas.

The mansion was purchased for $90,000 in 1911 by Winfield Scott, then the largest holder of real estate in the city of Fort Worth. Scott and his wife, Elizabeth, planned extensive remodeling of the mansion, turning the honeymoon cottage into a more formal Georgian Revival style home and clearly stamping it with their own identity. From then on, the mansion was no longer Thistle Hill but the Scott Home. Newspaper accounts estimated the remodeling cost at $100,000, though this figure was probably a slight exaggeration. The Scotts did hire the firm of Sanguinet and Staats to plan the remodeling.

Unfortunately, Scott died before the remodeling was complete enough to allow them occupancy, but the widowed Mrs. Scott lived there first with her son and then alone for over thirty-five years. At her death, her only son, Winfield, Jr., a black sheep with a ne'er-do-well reputation, is said to have auctioned many of her belongings and sold the house on the hill for a mere $17,500 in spite of its supposed value of $75,000. In truth, real estate was low then and the immediate neighborhood declining, no longer a prestigious residential area but not yet of commercial value. The low purchase price also accommodated the tax-free status of the purchaser, a charitable organization known as the Girls Service League.

The next occupants of the mansion were first high school girls from broken homes and then young working girls, and for them dormitory-like accommodations were created in the elegant home. The Girls Service League did some expedient remodeling often considered unfortunate—painting over unique wall treatments, for example—but their patchwork remodeling, dictated by limited financing, in many cases preserved historic elements of the house which might have been destroyed by a more thorough remodeling with an unlimited budget. Although they were forced to ignore needed repairs, the league must be credited with saving the house from destruction at a time when similar homes on Quality Hill were falling victim to progress and the wrecker's ball. Among the homes demolished were those owned by W. T. Waggoner himself and by Electra's brother, Guy Waggoner, both within sight of Thistle Hill.

In 1968, the league put Thistle Hill, still known as the Scott Home, up for sale. Their asking price was $325,000, an amount deemed necessary for the organization to continue its record of charity. It seemed that the last of Fort Worth's grand cattle baron mansions was destined to make way for progress. When the league moved out, the still-unsold house stood vacant for several years, its physical condition steadily deteriorating. However, a spirited citizens' group, known as Save-the-Scott Home, determinedly began a community-wide effort to raise enough money to save the old house. Their goal was to save the mansion as a classic example of the era, the people and the lifestyle that shaped Fort Worth as a city. Eventually, the league lowered the price, the citizens' group was successful in securing financing, and the Scott Home was saved.

Today the mansion, owned and operated by Texas Heritage, Inc., is open to the public for tours and private functions. Restoration of the house has not been done with the goal of recreating a period house, with untouchable rooms roped off to be viewed from a distance. Instead, the goal has been to create a building that can be used, and indeed today it is host to everything from weddings to spook houses. Restoration to the original 1904 condition has been impossible because of the extensive remodeling undertaken by the Scotts. The changes wrought by the Girls Service League, however, were more easily reversed, and the target of restoration has been to return the house to its 1912 state, approximating the technology available to the wealthy homeowner at that time.

Thistle Hill is a classic architectural example from the turn-of-the-century, when architecture was a means of expressing wealth, pride, ambition and self-satisfaction. Boasting stenciling and wall treatments more elaborate than found in similar grand homes, it is a tribute not to the Waggoner or Wharton or Scott families and fortunes but to a time, a place and a cattle baron heritage in the city that still calls itself Cowtown.

This, then, is the story of Thistle Hill.

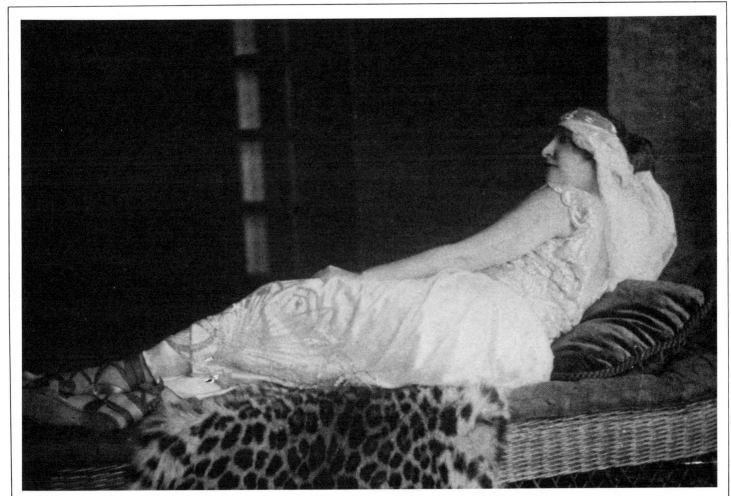

The Fabulous Electra

THISTLE HILL has always been known by the two ladies for whom it was home—Electra Waggoner Wharton and Elizabeth Simmons Scott. A. B. Wharton, Jr., has been casually mentioned by history only in conjunction with his wife, although the suspicion lingers that he was himself a person of some interest; after he and Electra divorced, he disappeared from Fort Worth history. Winfield Scott, unfortunately, died before he could occupy Thistle Hill, so although his money and, to some extent, his taste affected the massive remodeling, he himself is not associated with the mansion. Elizabeth Scott, however, lived there as a widow until her death in 1938.

If the mansion received its present character and dignity from Mrs. Scott, it received from the fabulous Electra the glamor that made it legendary. Electra was the daughter of W. T. Waggoner, a colorful and hard-driving man who arrived in North Central Texas as a youngster and led his first trail drive north at the age of sixteen. As much an empire builder as a cattleman, W.T. put every penny he earned into land, gradually increasing his holdings until by the turn of the century cattle with the well-known backwards DDD brand roamed on the largest ranch in Texas under one fence, a spread so vast it reached into six North Central Texas counties.

Colorful legends have attached themselves to the life and words of this cattleman who leased Indian lands from the Comanche chief Quanah Parker, helped organize the first cattle raisers' protective organization, played host to President T. R. Roosevelt at a wolf hunt, and once divided his property among his three children, giving them a total of approximately $6 million in land and livestock for a Christmas present. Supposedly, when oil was first discovered on Waggoner land, W.T. in disgust said he wanted none of the nasty stuff. What he needed was water for his cattle! That first hole was plugged with trash, and neighboring ranchers were invited to use the black goo for cattle dip. Yet he was a man careful with a penny: when he rode a train that was held up, the robber got little from W.T. and warned him that a man of his wealth should carry more money when traveling; another time, when a drummer, as salesmen were then called, offered fifty cents to anyone who would carry his bags from the station to the hotel, Waggoner volunteered. As they walked, the drummer noticed a huge mansion dominating the streets of the tiny town of Decatur. Curious, he asked who owned such a grand house. Waggoner said that it was his, and the drummer asked how he could afford such a house. Waggoner is supposed to have growled, "I carry my own bags."

Electra, so the legend goes, did not inherit her father's caution with money, but she was as determined and independent an individual as he. She and her two brothers, E. Paul and Guy, were the only survivors of five children born to W.T. and his wife, Ella. In spite of his hard-driving ambition and his sometimes gruff ways, Waggoner doted on his only daughter. Her name, famous in Greek mythology, in this case is nothing more than a feminization of her maternal grandfather's name, Electius, and a reflection of the popularity of unusual names in the early 1880s.

From the time she was very young, Electra lived in a mansion. W.T. and his father, Dan, built the mansion in Decatur, so admired by the traveling salesman, in 1882 so that the family could live in town, though W.T. continued to ranch far to the north. The sixteen-room home, called El Castile, featured massive hand-carved exterior doors, walls two feet thick and ceilings eighteen feet high, some with fresco paintings done by a Paris artist. There were door hinges of carved brass and an intricately handcarved newel post. From its upstairs porches and balconies, the Waggoners could look beyond the town of Decatur to the Texas prairies from which came the fortune to build the house. El Castile still stands today in Decatur.

If Electra was raised in luxury at El Castile, she was

also raised as a cattleman's daughter. She was close to her father, and he taught her to shoot and to ride like an Indian. Cowboys on the Waggoner spread called her the "Princess of the Panhandle." But the family—probably Electra's mother, Ella, who had lived in a log cabin, worked in the field, and hidden from marauding Comanches—wanted the girl to become a lady. In 1897, at the age of fifteen, Electra Waggoner was sent East to finishing school.

In 1900 she returned, a properly turned out young lady, to a round of parties and visiting and steady beaux. Her comings and goings were faithfully reported in the local newspaper, the *Wise County Messenger*. Typical of her parties was an elaborate Japanese tea for which El Castile was decorated with fans, oriental floral arrangements, and Japanese lanterns. Electra greeted her guests wearing a floral Japanese robe. Another time, she gave a party to which only girls were invited; half came dressed in Napoleonic costumes, the others in Martha Washington-style dresses. Clearly, by the time she was mistress of Thistle Hill, Electra was an experienced hostess.

Sent on a world tour to discourage her wedding plans to a local swain—some say he was one of the ranch hands—she met Albert Buckman Wharton, Jr., a Philadelphia socialite, and fell gloriously in love with him in the mountains of Nepal. She returned home with an outrageous butterfly tattooed on her leg and wonderful stories of the man who had swept her off her feet.

That year, she had an unusual birthday gift: a town was named for her. The town of Electra had been generally known as Waggoner Switch, but residents received their mail addressed to Beaver. When they petitioned for one name, W.T. declined to have a town named Waggoner, so residents honored the eighteen-year-old Electra on her birthday. Later, in 1911, when a major oil discovery was made on Waggoner property, the town boomed overnight then rapidly shrank again in population. But Electra herself was already long gone to Thistle Hill.

Electra and A. B. Wharton, Jr., were married in June 1902. The bride's trousseau was from Paris, and she wore a rosepoint veil brought from Europe, where it had been worn by the Hapsburgs. (The veil has since been worn by her niece and namesake, Electra Waggoner Biggs, and by Mrs. Biggs' two daughters.)

The newly married Whartons left for an extended honeymoon in Europe.

Wharton bought the land at 1509 Pennsylvania from a Fort Worth resident named J. S. Zane-Cetti for $25,000. Building plans were announced December 31, 1902, by which time the newlyweds were back in Decatur. With their infant son, they moved into the new house in 1904. Later, W.T. built a house catty-corner to the northwest, and Electra's brother, Guy, built next door to Thistle Hill. Quality Hill became a Waggoner family enclave.

The years in Thistle Hill established Electra's international reputation for lavish living and glamor. Legend says that she was the first to spend $20,000 on a one-day shopping spree at Neiman Marcus in Dallas; she returned the next day to spend almost as much for things she had overlooked on the first trip. Fresh flowers were delivered to her home daily, and the latest clothes arrived from Paris and New York for her to consider—she would never try on a garment already tried by someone else and she never wore anything twice. The closets at Thistle Hill bulged with shoes—once in her life she was said to own 350 pairs—and furs and fine gowns.

As a couple, the Whartons entertained with great style during their years in Thistle Hill, and local newspapers, more prone in that day to report social events in detail, were full of what happened at the mansion on the hill.

In 1906, for instance, there was a "phantom dance" for Halloween: guests were pillowcased and sheeted and the only lighting came from glowing pumpkins. The same year an old-fashioned candy pull made the kitchen "a very lively place" and an al fresco party on the verandah offered card games, professional vaudeville performers and luncheon for two hundred guests "both married and unmarried folks." And New Year's saw 160 friends at the house from 5–8 P.M. The ballroom "was elaborately decorated with smilax and tinsel and a large Christmas tree was the centerpiece." Even in 1909, the year before they vacated the house, the Whartons entertained lavishly, receiving New Year's callers in the afternoon and serving an evening supper for seventy guests. Following supper, there were six cotillions, presumably in the third-floor ballroom "which had the appearance of a bower of vines and roses."

Newspaper records of these parties provide a clear picture of upper class entertaining at that time. Costume figures or dances were popular: the Whartons gave Indian figures, military figures, a North Pole figure (ladies wore ermine). Lavish decorations set the tone for what today we would call theme parties, and there were fresh flowers used in abundance—cherry blossoms and wisteria for Japanese parties, lilies and palms for New Year's, with the fireplace filled with ferns and the mantel covered with moss and leaves or, another year, long-stemmed American beauty roses in vases and jardinieres. On one Fourth of July the house was draped in red, white and blue bunting, with tiny flags on the porches and fences, and thousands of dollars worth of fireworks were set off. Nothing was done modestly or without flair.

The newspaper reports always refer correctly to Mr. and Mrs. Wharton, but A.B. Wharton, Jr., remains a mysterious figure during those times. Apparently he was locally prominent during the marriage, perhaps due in part to his ownership of the first automobile agency in Fort Worth. On their return from Europe, he and Electra had shocked everyone in Decatur by arriving in a car. Later, Wharton opened Fort Worth Auto & Livery. The firm sold Franklins and Winstons and, according to their advertisements, offered both

rental and repair service. In 1904, he had established an automobile club in Fort Worth, and by 1906 city records showed a total of ninety cars in Fort Worth; Wharton owned five of those. The city had a speed limit of seven m.p.h., though this slow speed often caused overheating of early automobiles. In 1907, both M. R. Sanguinet and Guy Waggoner were cited for exceeding that limit. In 1911, a car owned but not driven by Wharton won a five-mile race at the fairgrounds.

Evidence of Wharton's interest in automobiles may be found at Thistle Hill. The carriage house has a gas pump and its own storage tank, probably installed by Wharton.

Wharton's other interests apparently involved horses and dogs. He owned and showed horses with some success, according to news reports, and at least once attended field trials at the U.S. Field Club with dogs from his personal kennel. There is shadowy photographic evidence that a building existed on the southeast corner of the property during the Whartons' residence. It may have housed automobiles, dogs or horses. The structure was demolished during the Scott remodeling.

When W.T. Waggoner made his munificent gift to his children at Christmas 1910, the Whartons announced their intention to build a home on their ranch property near Vernon, Texas and sell Thistle Hill. Wharton, so accounts went, would devote his time to their ranch and cattle. The Whartons did divide their time between the ranch home, which Electra called Zacaweista (an Indian word for long grasses), and the Waggoner home in Fort Worth until 1919 when they divorced.

Electra later bought Shadow Lawn, a seven-acre estate in Dallas, where she solidified her reputation as a playgirl and hostess. Shadow Lawn was furnished with a half-million dollar's worth of art from Europe—a Persian carpet valued at $42,000, a specially designed banquet table with matching inlaid Venetian cabinet, an imported marble chest that cost more than most people's houses. In some rooms, so the story went, fifteen coats of paint were required to achieve the exact shade desired.

Electra's parties at Shadow Lawn became legendary. The guest list included national politicians, movie idols, and socialites. She delighted in entertaining eastern dignitaries and showing them a bit of the Wild West, once shooting a six-shooter through the dining room ceiling and another time taking the whole party to Zacaweista in time to see a gusher blow in.

Electra married twice more but in 1925, her health having been poor for several years, she died of cirrhosis of the liver at the early age of forty-three. Even in death she made headlines: her brother, Guy, in St. Louis when informed of her impending demise, chartered a Pacific and Atlantic train and made the trip of over one thousand miles to her deathbed in New York in the record time of twenty hours and twenty-three minutes. It was said to have cost young Waggoner nine thousand dollars.

Perhaps the Greek meaning of Electra's name was, after all, appropriate, for she blazed across Texas like a legend. Yet, strangely, she was perhaps more notorious than unique, for she was not the only second generation of a cattle baron's family to live a life of luxury and extravagance. Not only her home but also her lifestyle speak of a time, a place, and a people who went from poverty to incredible wealth in two generations.

13

Elizabeth Scott

A Standard of Style

NO TWO LADIES could have had more contrasting styles than Electra Waggoner Wharton and Elizabeth Simmons Scott. Where Electra blazed a legend of glamor, Elizabeth set a quiet standard of style.

Unlike the first mistress of Thistle Hill, Elizabeth had little exposure to cowboys until she married cattleman Winfield Scott. The story is told that her first glimpse of cowboys came when the Simmons family, displaced from their Southern home by the Civil War, traveled from Galveston, their point of embarkation, to Weatherford, where the girl's father would practice medicine. At the stage stop at Salado, Elizabeth, then a child of nine or ten, saw a group of cowboys and was quite taken aback by their rough and rowdy ways.

The Simmons family settled in Parker County in 1870, during the years when that county was the target of many raids by the Comanches and Kiowas. Yet Elizabeth had a sheltered and fairly genteel upbringing, somehow insulated from the frontier which surrounded her. She was educated in Weatherford, where the family was socially prominent, until her teens when she spent a year at the Ursuline Convent in Dallas. Apparently, Elizabeth Simmons' young life went along smoothly in the pattern of upper middle class, well educated and carefully protected girls until, at the age of twenty-one, she met Winfield Scott who was visiting in Weatherford.

Scott at the time was a widower, ranching in the area of Colorado City, but he had already led a more colorful and certainly less protected life than his wife-to-be. Born in Kentucky and raised in Missouri, he had come to Tarrant County as a young man. His first job, so the story goes, was chopping wood along the banks of the Trinity River. Ambitious and determined, he soon saved $500 with which he bought land; he borrowed money to stock the land with cattle.

Having established himself, Scott returned to Missouri to marry his childhood sweetheart, O'Delia Colley, to whom he had written countless love letters. Evidence suggests that Scott was uneducated and illiterate and that the letters were written at his dictation by someone else; after their marriage, O'Delia taught him to read and write. They lived at the corner of Taylor and Texas streets, in what is now downtown Fort Worth, and Scott became a fairly well known cattleman. Life must have seemed in order to him until O'Delia died three weeks after the birth of their first child, a daughter named Georgia.

Overcome by grief, Scott allowed his mother to take the child back to Missouri to raise; he left Fort Worth for Colorado City, to begin a new life. Five years later in 1883, he met Elizabeth Simmons.

Theirs was a year-long engagement, with her family expressing some anxiety about her moving beyond the pale of society to a rough cattle town like Colorado City. But Scott, in what might have been an omen for the future, bought the only brick house in the city and, although the house was only a year old, spent $10,000 remodeling it for his bride. Though they lived there for six years after their marriage and European honeymoon, the impression is that Elizabeth was once again sheltered from the frontier and never really lived among cattlemen as Electra had.

Drought brought hard times to Colorado City and the cattle industry, and Scott decided in 1889 to move back to Fort Worth, then a growing city boasting much construction, a public school system, an ice plant, flour mills, the Fort Worth Panthers baseball team and the Spring Palace exhibit of Texas agriculture. The Scotts bought a home on Lamar and Fifth streets, property which much later Mrs. Scott donated to the YMCA and which is still the location of the downtown YMCA today. Unlike Thistle Hill, this house had a third-floor ballroom clearly designed for that purpose.

Winfield Scott diversified his interests, investing heavily in downtown property while also increasing his ranch holdings. (He called one of his ranches The Scottland.) He owned several hotels and the legendary White Elephant Saloon, site of the famous gunfight between Luke Short and Longhair Jim Courtright. In 1908 he was the largest individual subscriber, at $10,000, to a packing house project, and in 1911 his numerous remodeling projects were cited as a major example of the growth of Fort Worth.

Elizabeth meanwhile spent her time entertaining, taking care of her husband and becoming friends, to some extent, with his daughter, Georgia. Retrieving Georgia from Scott's mother had proved difficult, and daughter and stepmother had a rocky relationship, sometimes friends and sometimes bitter enemies, the rest of their lives.

Winfield and Elizabeth's only child, Winfield Scott, Jr., was born in 1901. They had then been married for seventeen years; Elizabeth was nearing forty, Scott was well into his fifties, and the infant's half sister, Georgia, was married with an infant son of her own. Elizabeth was determined that this child, who would have the important task of carrying on the Scott name, have every advantage that Scott had missed in his own youth. He was spoiled and indulged from the moment of his birth, and he grew up to squander a fortune, marry eight wives, spend some time in federal prison for drug violations and break his mother's heart.

Toward the end of the first decade of this century, the Scotts decided to retire to St. Louis, a city Elizabeth had visited often. Scott purchased a large home there, and Elizabeth established the family, participating in the life of high society in the city, sending her child to the right schools and generally putting down roots. But after nearly two years, Scott decided to return to Fort Worth where he had so many holdings. His decision was accelerated by the news that the Whartons had offered their home for sale. Scott, who had admired Thistle Hill for years, paid $90,000 for the mansion.

What was first conceived as minor remodeling turned

A view of the pergola.

into work so extensive that only some rooms on the third floor and in the basement of Thistle Hill were left untouched. This was to be their retirement home, the last remodeling that they would ever undertake, the home in which Winfield and Elizabeth would grow old together while raising young Winfield to carry on the family name. During the long nine months of remodeling, Elizabeth and her child commuted from St. Louis; Scott himself remained mostly in Fort Worth, living at the Worth Hotel.

Winfield Scott died before he could move into his mansion. His final illness began with a sore on his nose, but evidence suggests that he was also exhausted, worn out by the hard work of building his fortune. At his death, he was Fort Worth's heaviest taxpayer, worth an estimated $4 million, $2.5 million of it in Fort Worth real estate. His biggest project, the construction of a new hotel to be called The Winfield, was not completed until 1921, when it was named The Texas. It stands today, completely renovated, as the Hyatt Regency/Fort Worth.

Elizabeth Scott and her ten-year-old son moved into Thistle Hill. The boy had inherited upwards of $3 million at his father's death, making him the richest boy in Fort Worth. Elizabeth and Georgia were the only other heirs, but Georgia's inheritance was slight and she sued. A bitter and lengthy court battle followed, ensuring the end of whatever kind feelings had existed between Georgia and her stepmother. Under terms of the settlement, Georgia shared equally in the inheritance with her half brother and received approximately one-third of the estate.

In spite of the scandal and distress of lawsuits, Elizabeth Scott was a gracious and serene mistress of Thistle Hill. She went to New York annually to buy new gowns, especially one for The Assembly Ball, and she participated actively in her community, serving on the board for the Southwest Exposition and Fat Stock Show, donating to the Carnegie Library, holding life membership in the Women's Club and River Crest Country Club.

Elizabeth entertained often at Thistle Hill, and she was noted especially for her unique table settings. She had complete sets of china, crystal and linens in many colors and served on them elaborate dinners of several courses, a much more formal style of entertaining than that practiced by Electra. Whether entertaining at home or moving about in Fort Worth society, she always wore the diamond "dog collar" necklace that Winfield had bought for her on their Paris honeymoon.

It would be fair to say that Thistle Hill owes its architectural and social importance to the first twenty years of its existence—Electra's years and the first decade of Elizabeth's occupancy. Though she lived there until her death in 1938, Elizabeth Scott was neither happy nor socially active in her later years, and the few changes she made to the house tended to disrupt its harmony. An attempted burglary sparked a fear which led her to install bars on some windows and often to lock herself in the master bedroom area; in her last years, she was prevailed upon to have a caretaker stay with her in the house, and young Winfield periodically lived with her, though his presence could not have cheered her much. She did find great joy in her only granddaughter, a child name Winifred.

After Elizabeth's death, Winfield Jr. is thought to have auctioned or sold directly many of the house's furnishings, though occasionally a piece has turned up in the possession of a descendant or close friend, casting doubt on the auction story. But in 1940, having spent both his own and his mother's fortune, Winfield Jr. sold the mansion. The years of its private ownership had ended.

The tea house, adorned with plants, was a cool and comfortable retreat from the heat of a Texas summer.

The Girls Service League

FROM 1940 UNTIL 1968, Thistle Hill was owned and occupied by the Girls Service League, a philanthropic organization dedicated to providing homes for underprivileged girls. In addition to Thistle Hill, the league also leased several houses, among them a former home of Electra's father, W. T. Waggoner, on Summit Avenue. The league's central offices were in Thistle Hill until 1958.

The league purchased the house in 1940 for $17,500, an admitted bargain price for property appraised at $75,000. But by then the wealthy families of Fort Worth were deserting Quality Hill to move west to the newer neighborhoods of River Crest and Westover Hills. Tax considerations further complicated the purchase price of the Scott property. Even the $17,500 price, however, was monumental for this charitable organization. Financing for the purchase was arranged through a prominent Fort Worth citizen, J. Marvin Leonard, acting on behalf of a trust. The league repaid the loan in slightly over four years.

Winfield Scott, Jr., had moved out of the family home after his mother's death in 1938, and Thistle Hill stood vacant for about two years. When the Girls Service League took possession, their first act was a thorough housecleaning. Windows were washed, ornate woodwork waxed and polished, everything dusted and cleaned. When the house sparkled, the league held an open house, with the season's debutantes serving as hostesses. The open house was so successful and drew such a crowd that it was extended to a second day;

in two days, over twelve hundred people toured the mansion.

But then it was down to business as a boarding house for Thistle Hill. Dormitory space was created to allow about thirty-five girls to sleep on the second floor. The third floor was made into dressing rooms since the fire code forbade sleeping there. At first, the house was home to underprivileged high school girls in need of shelter; during World War II, it provided much-needed living space for young working girls, many of them involved in the war effort. No matter the age of the girls, however, they were expected to follow a rather strict set of house rules about men as visitors, attending the church of their choice, being present at meals, helping with running the house. There was, said one former resident, a family atmosphere and that included good food served at a big dining table where everyone ate together.

One woman who lived there in 1943–44 while working at Consolidated Vultee (now General Dynamics) recalled the house as a wonderful, romantic place to live, with "a staircase so grand you could dream." She remembered particularly the elegant gardens and

the maple bedroom and recalled that the girls were well aware of the need to be careful of a house so grand, though there was no talk of historic preservation and they were never told the history of the two families who had lived in Thistle Hill.

The same woman recalled that the girls joined the USO and often entertained soldiers and sailors at Sunday dinner. The young men, she said, were equally impressed with the house. The highlight of her memories was the wedding of a resident, a blind girl who worked at the Lighthouse for the Blind and married a blind co-worker. "I was her bridal attendant and helped her down the staircase—we came down the center, of course—and I was terrified that we would both fall."

After the war, there was less need of housing for working girls, and the league again housed teenagers in the mansion. But by the late 1960s other properties had been given to the league to meet their housing needs. Meanwhile, at Thistle Hill, major structural problems, in large part due to lack of maintenance and the need for modernization, were appearing. In 1968, the league vacated the house. In 1969, they held a Green and Gold Tea there in celebration of the fiftieth anniversary of the league—gold for fifty years of the past and green for the new growth of the future. It was the last Girls Service League function to be held in the house.

Standard opinion for many years was that the league made practical but unfortunate changes at Thistle Hill. Such a view overlooks two ways in which the Girls Service League was essential to the preservation of this historic house. By their very occupancy of the mansion, the league saved it from demolition at a time when the mansions on Quality Hill were falling to the wrecker's ball like pins to a bowling ball. The homes of Electra's father, W.T., and her brother, Guy, were both among those razed. But Thistle Hill was owned and occupied and thus, even though the property was zoned G-Commercial, it was saved.

Further, the league's lack of funds ironically proved a boon to historic preservation. Because they had no money, the league took the cheapest route in converting and maintaining the house—they painted and covered, but they never moved walls or made major changes. The canvas wall covering in the library, for instance, was painted over; the paint can be removed,

the original fabric cleaned and restored, and the stenciling revealed. In the mahogany bedroom, the wallpaper was painted over; a well-financed remodeling project would have called for stripping off the wallpaper. Instead, it remains visible to serve as an example for preservationists. The league's very lack of money kept them from compromising the historic integrity of the house; had they been graced with unlimited funds, they might have undertaken remodeling which would have made any kind of restoration impossible. It's interesting to remember in that light that the extensive remodeling done by the Scotts in 1911 has made it impossible to restore the house to its original 1903 condition.

The house did suffer some damage during the league's residence, principally because the organization lacked the funds for heavy maintenance. The roof leaked and was patched but could not be replaced, a major improvement since undertaken. During the period after the league vacated the house, when it stood empty, there was substantial water damage to areas on the second and third floors. Similarly, a downspout into the ground, presumably from a nonfunctioning cistern,

Handmade Planter

saturated the earth, causing damage to the north porch. This damage was increased by overgrown vegetation which also held the moisture. In addition, the house showed signs of careless painting around windows, thoughtless installation of electrical work, and damaged plaster.

But the Girls Service League should not be criticized for failure to recognize the importance of historic preservation. Preservation was not, until the 1960s, a concern to many people in this country. And perhaps it was fortuitous that the league chose to vacate the house and place it on the market at a time when individuals and cities were just beginning to recognize the importance of saving historic structures. The league, albeit unwittingly, had done its part for preservation by saving the house from demolition. Restoration would come next.

Save-the-Scott Home

THAT THISTLE HILL was saved for Fort Worth was a miracle, against all odds. When the shabby mansion was put up for sale by the Girls Service League, its future was uncertain but seemed bound to one of two possibilities: demolition to make room for one or more commercial buildings or conversion to commercial use itself.

About that time, the Junior League of Fort Worth and the Amon Carter Foundation cooperated on a survey of historic buildings in Fort Worth. With the Tarrant County Historical Commission, they arranged school bus tours of historic sites, distributed maps, planned dedication ceremonies, and researched the history necessary for applications for historic markers. Thistle Hill, then known as the Scott Home, was one of twelve sites designated as significant and worthy of preservation.

Such recognition did little for the mansion on the real estate market. But in September 1974, a loosely organized group, spurred by the suggestion of a longtime Fort Worth resident, met to discuss buying the property. There was no historic preservation society in the city at the time, and this was a group of beginners, mostly women and only a few businessmen. Nonetheless, the idea of failure never occurred to them. They met in the office of a local architect who arranged to provide office space, and the Save-the-Scott movement was born.

Sure that everybody in Fort Worth would leap to join their cause, they began to solicit memberships.

Their first big effort was to sponsor a membership booth at the city's annual Oktoberfest. But it was a pillar-to-post campaign. They would put out a big mailing to gain members, and then have a fund-raiser to pay for the mailing. What they found, to their surprise, was that the people of Fort Worth, those with moderate means, did almost leap to join their cause: there was a flood of ten-dollar donations, but there were no large donations from major companies. Meanwhile, all those small donations from bighearted people went into escrow, to be returned to the donors should the effort not meet success.

The group adopted a motto: "We the willing led by the unknowing are doing the impossible for the ungrateful. We have done so much for so long with so little we are now qualified to do anything with nothing."

By 1975, the Save-the-Scott was incorporated and negotiating a lease with the Girls Service League. No one among them realized the impossibility of raising $1000 for rent every month. After Save-the-Scott occupied the house, eviction seemed inevitable on several occasions as the rent money grew more and more difficult to raise, but the group remained ever optimistic.

The limestone pillars of the front porch, taken from the east.

Meanwhile, their first chore on moving in was to mop the floors of pigeon droppings. For over seven years, pigeons had been the only occupants of the house. The core of ten volunteers who anchored the Save-the-Scott movement found themselves more and more protective of the mansion. If the house was rented for a function, at least one of them was present to see that no nail holes were put in the walls, no glass rings left on polished wood surfaces. When the opportunity came to have the home shown as a Designers Showhouse, the group refused, in spite of a healthy sum of money involved. Giving the designers carte blanche to work with the walls of the house, even staple fabric and perhaps remove existing wall covers, was not in their plan of preservation. They found their dedication becoming all-consuming.

Help, both financial and organizational, came from the Texas Historical Commission and from the the Community Development program of HUD, the federal urban development agency. A controversy arose with the City of Fort Worth over the legality of using government community development funds for historic preservation. Backed by an opinion from HUD Director Carla Hill in their favor, the Save-the-Scott group sued the city manager, the city attorney and the city government; they also petitioned HUD to stop community development funds, thereby tying up federal money to the city. The city withdrew. In effect, the group had fought City Hall and won, though unanimously they praised the support given them by the city government and explained that the legal difficulties were no more than a matter of interpretation.

Help came to the group also from small local organizations: the Board of Realtors adopted the cause and gave them a representative to negotiate the purchase of the house; the *Fort Worth Star-Telegram* sold prints of a drawing of the house done by their famous editorial cartoonist, Harold Maples; the auxiliary to the local Greek church held a bake sale; the Old Spaghetti Warehouse restaurant turned their opening over to the Save-the-Scott, allowing the group to sell tickets and to take all the profits as a donation; Boy Scouts cleaned the yard, and stereotypical little old ladies in tennis shoes hoed the garden. Many of those who worked so hard to save the mansion traced their dedication to childhood memories of driving by the grandest house they could ever imagine. It was a shirt-sleeves effort, and it caught the public fancy.

In 1976, the Save-the-Scott group had to evacuate the mansion because they could not raise $375,000. They had, however, raised a remarkable $200,000 in their pillar-to-post campaign. Undaunted, they moved their headquarters to a board member's basement laundry room and kept on working, convinced that the ouster was temporary. A big boost came with a grant from the Texas Historical Commission; another with a sizeable gift from Electra Waggoner Biggs, namesake-descendant of Electra Waggoner Wharton.

Throughout the long negotiations, the Girls Service League was firmly on the side of the Save-the-Scott. Their real estate agent, dedicated to the preservation of the mansion, once presented three contracts to the league but advised considering only one: that from the Save-the-Scott. The other two involved commercial use of the property, including one from a group of investors who would refurbish the house (without preserving its authenticity) as a nightclub. Among the many who wanted to buy the property was an individual who said he wanted to raise his son in a grand home.

The Girls Service League received undeserved negative publicity during the negotiation with the Save-the-Scott group. They were, in effect, criticized for not coming down on their price in the interests of historic preservation. Finally, the exasperated president of the league reminded a newspaperman that the league had, after all, been preserving the house for thirty-six years. But those close to the negotiations, the active members of the Save-the-Scott movement, knew that the league's own charitable priorities argued against a dramatic decrease in their asking price for the house. Nonetheless, they did reduce it well over $100,000.

In August 1976, the Save-the-Scott organization got the key to the mansion. Dedication ceremonies followed, attended by local and state officials. But it was less the dignitaries that gave significance to the event than the people of Fort Worth. It was their house, and they belonged there.

The name of the house was changed back to Thistle Hill, as it was first called, and the process of restoration began.

Thistle Hill ~ The House

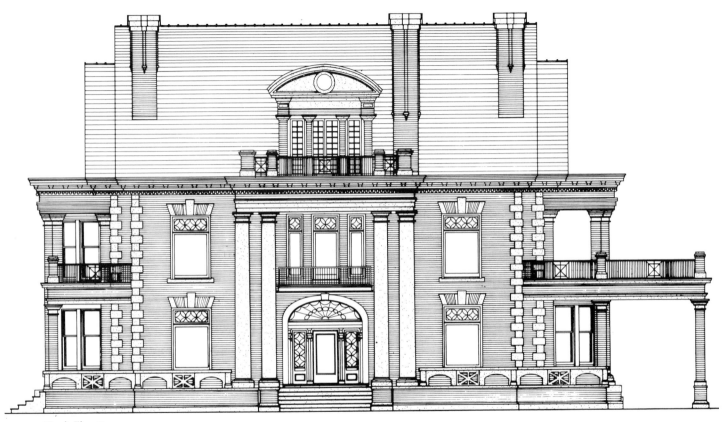

North Elevation.

The Exterior

THISTLE HILL is sometimes called a "honeymoon cottage," a name probably given it because it was the first home shared by Electra Waggoner and A. B. Wharton, Jr., after their marriage. The word cottage was often used in the early twentieth century to describe a second home, and it may be that ranch property in North Central Texas was considered the primary residence of Electra and her bridegroom. But its size and grandeur make Thistle Hill anything but a cottage. The only cottage-like element of the house, as it was designed in 1903, was its informality.

The firm of Sanguinet and Staats, designers of Thistle Hill, was one of the most successful and influential architectural firms in Texas, with offices, at various times, in Dallas, Houston, Waco and San Antonio. Noted for both commercial and private properties, they designed many buildings still standing today in Fort Worth. Among them are the Marshall Sanguinet home on Collinwood, the Mitchell-Schoonover house on Eighth Avenue, the Baldridge house on Crestline Road, the Hyatt Regency Hotel (built as the Winfield Hotel and known for many years as the Texas), the W. T. Waggoner Building, the Burkburnett Building, the Flatiron, the Knights of Pythias Hall and the City National Bank Building.

Sanguinet and Staats designed Thistle Hill, perhaps at the request of the newlyweds or W. T. Waggoner, in the Colonial Revival style, which was characterized by the almost exclusive use of wood for decorative elements and creates a structure less formal than one decorated with marble or wrought iron. In its informality, Thistle Hill was initially planned for a rather casual lifestyle.

The Scotts, however, brought a more formal lifestyle to the mansion, and the architectural changes they made obliterated the elements of the Colonial

Revival style, replacing wooden adornments with the wrought iron and stone decorative elements of Georgian Revival, a cleaner, less decorated and more formal architectural style. By converting the house to the Georgian Revival style, the Scotts not only stamped their personal identity on it but also created a house unusual to the Southwest, where Colonial Revival homes were much more common than Georgian Revival.

The house was built as a basic brick structure decorated with several wooden elements. The roof was of wood shingle, painted green, and two dormer windows, characteristic of Colonial Revival, were set in the roof on either side of a wooden broken pediment adornment. A porch, with a wooden balustrade painted white, encircled the entire front of the house at the second floor level, and the house featured two semicircular open porches on either side.

For many years it was thought that the six two-story stone pillars on the front porch were original to the house. They are of limestone, each seven feet in circumference and carved of one piece. Tradition said that the pillars were carved in Indiana and brought to Fort Worth in special boxcars. From the railroad yards, specially constructed covered wagons transported the pillars to the building site. The probability that Indiana limestone was used in these columns is increased by the fact that at the time no quarry in Texas could have handled an order for columns of such massive size. However, more recent examination of structural and photographic evidence suggests that the original columns were of fluted wood. In that case, the limestone columns were probably part of the Scott remodeling.

Limestone is used extensively as decoration on the exterior of the house, and analysis has proven all except the columns to be Texas leuders limestone, probably from the Abilene area. It is used in quoins (decorative motifs at the corners of the building), and a courser of limestone defines the floor level of the house. The entire building also has an approximately two-foot footing of limestone. In the 1912 remodeling, Sanguinet and Staats made extensive use of limestone, adding, for example, the banister on the front verandah and the side panels down the front steps. Like many other touches in the remodeling, this use of a previously used material assured that the remodeled house was in harmony with the original structure.

The only outbuilding original to the construction of

Carriage House

the house is the carriage house. Since A. B. Wharton, Jr., was Fort Worth's first automobile dealer and brought an automobile to the city as early as 1903, this carriage house was probably used as much for automobiles as horses. It is equipped with a gas tank and pump, but it also was built with a cooling or drying yard for horses. Inside, it features an unusual and innovative block and tackle system by which hay was loaded to a second-story storage level, then fed down a chute to the waiting horses.

The Scott remodeling brought dramatic changes to the exterior of the house and to the grounds. Essentially, they stripped the house to a brick block and began again.

The wooden decorative elements were replaced with the tile, marble and stone characteristic of Georgian Revival. The wooden shingle roof was replaced with a roof of green glazed terra cotta tile, though the original roof was left on the carriage house where it can be seen today. The dormer windows were removed, making the roof surface cleaner, and the wooden pediment replaced with an inset of Italian marble and limestone which repeated motifs at the top of the limestone columns. The large balcony with its wooden balustrade was stripped from the building to be re-

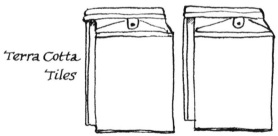

Terra Cotta Tiles

An ivy-covered post on the east side of the house, and a side view of the front pillars.

placed with a short, wrought iron railing placed directly over the front door. The circular bays were removed and rebuilt in brick and enclosed downstairs and upstairs on the east, creating a solarium and bay off the dining room downstairs and becoming part of the master bedroom upstairs. The dining room bay matched the already-existing bay in the game/music room and gave a certain symmetry to the house's exterior.

For the Whartons, the grounds of the house, though well maintained, were of less importance. For Mrs. Scott, the exterior of the house was an integral part of the overall dwelling, and she added not only the formal garden and the brick privacy fence characteristic of the Georgian Revival style but also outdoor structures which were suited to outdoor living in Texas. Both the pergola and the tea house were built during the Scotts' renovation.

The pergola is actually neither Colonial nor Georgian Revival in style but more typical of the arts and crafts movement of the post-Victorian period, a movement characterized by its use of exposed natural materials and its demonstration of craftsmanlike technique. A lattice-covered pillar-lined walk forty feet long, the

The tea house at the west edge of the property.

pergola sits to the west of the mansion, beyond the porte cochere. Mrs. Scott had jasmine and climbing roses planted to almost cover the frame of the structure.

The tea house sits at the end of the pergola, on the far west edge of the property. Built of red pressed brick with limestone copings, this building was built with a green tile roof, a wooden deck and a patterned

brick floor. Ceiling hooks indicate that the original structure had a hanging swing and several hanging plants. Both the pergola and the tea house would have enabled the Scott family to move their general living to the outdoors on hot summer nights when the mansion itself would still be stuffy but its hilltop setting, then not surrounded by city as today, would afford a breeze. By late evening, the breeze might have cooled the house sufficiently for the occupants to return, and the next day, when the outdoors might begin to be steamy, the high ceilings and thick walls of the house would keep it cool until past midday.

Two other outdoor structures on the property reflect the need to conserve every drop of precious water. Both Electra Waggoner Wharton and the Scotts were, after all, ranching people, well aware of the value of water in Texas. The structures are a water tower and a well cover. The well, sitting adjacent to the kitchen area of the house, was probably a cistern, with rainwater draining directly into it. The Whartons had it covered with a one-story well house with a shingle roof, matching the house, and walls of open

The three-story water tower, probably built around 1905, is no longer standing, although the foundation may be seen.

lattice work, painted white, which would have corresponded nicely with the balustrade of the house in their day. Mrs. Scott replaced that well house with a canopy of ironwork.

The water tower was a large, three-story structure probably built around 1905. Situated on a raised brick and concrete platform, it began with a one-story square red brick base from which a six-sided frame shaft rose. This shaft was covered with green wood shingles and topped with a white cupola surrounded by a balustrade. With its green wood shingles and white balustrade, the design of the water tower reflects the Colonial Revival origins of the house itself. The structure sat at the rear of the property, near Pruitt street.

Mrs. Scott's formal gardens lay in the southeast corner of the property, but the entire grounds of the mansion were carefully landscaped during both the Wharton and the Scott residencies. Larkspur, violets and petunias would have bloomed in the beds, and ivy covered the walls of the house itself.

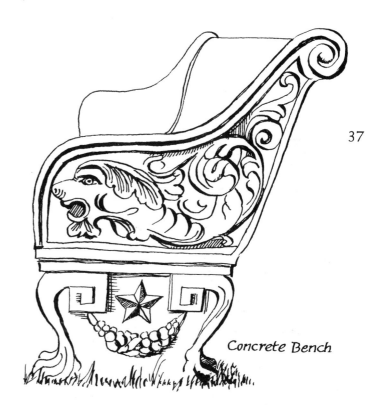

37

Concrete Bench

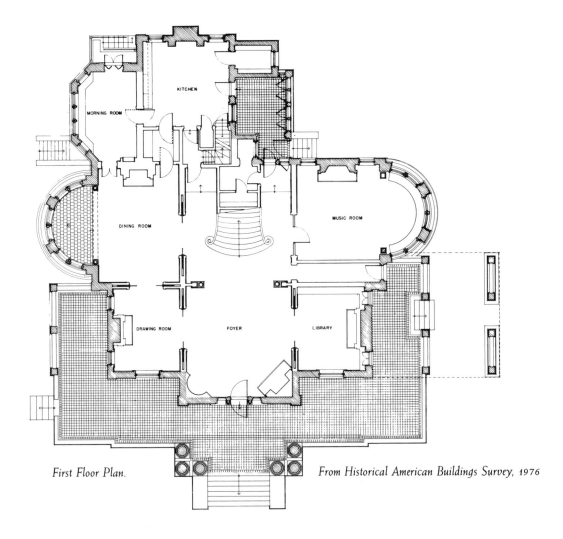

38

First Floor Plan.

From Historical American Buildings Survey, 1976

The Interior

THE FOYER ♣ Guests entered the Wharton residence through a leaded glass door with an arched fanlight which repeats the semicircular motif found throughout the house. Inside, they stood in a huge foyer dominated by a massive staircase. From one point just inside the front door, it is possible to see all five fireplaces in the downstairs of the house. Each fireplace is architecturally unique, but none was ever wood-burning. Instead each burned gas, although coal may also have been used.

The fireplace in the foyer is of green tile, echoing the green of the roof. Monumental in scale and set catty-corner in the room, it is typical of the arts and crafts style found throughout the house. Also significant are its combination of materials—tile and oak—and its mantel which slants from the front down toward the wall.

The foyer is of white English oak, with seven-foot wainscoting and a ceiling of decorative oak panels. The oak was ordered, custom cut, from Saint Louis, as was all the hardware on the doors and gates in the house and grounds. The walls above the wainscoting and the ceiling area within the panels were covered with a fabric-backed wall covering. The foyer can be closed off from the major downstairs rooms by sliding oak doors. The door jambs are framed by beaded molding, also typical of the arts and crafts style. Hardware to hang portiers exists at all of these sliding doors. As befit the tasteful house of the day, in Electra's time the wood, including the floor, would have been highly polished.

We cannot be absolutely sure how Electra used the foyer or how she had it decorated, but photographs demonstrate that Mrs. Scott used it more as living space than as a reception area. Less formal than the drawing room adjacent to it, the foyer served as a gathering place for family and casual visitors, much like a family room today. It was filled, almost clut-

This view of the foyer shows that Mrs. Scott used the space as a sitting room, filled with furniture and knickknacks.

A view through the foyer into the more formal parlor or drawing room.

42

A view through the foyer into the library.

tered, with furniture—probably a round table covered with an embroidered cloth and decorated with bric-a-brac and family photographs, a piano and bench, a tall clock, several chairs, a smoking stand, some large bronze figures and urns, and, of course, the radiators which kept the room warm in winter. Probably many of the furnishings were oriental in style, including the rugs. The wall sconces found in the room today are original.

Both Electra Wharton and Elizabeth Scott would have used new furniture throughout the house. Wealthy homes of the period were not characterized by an evident appreciation of antiques. Wealth afforded both mistresses of Thistle Hill the opportunity to buy new, and neither would have had furniture made prior to 1900.

THE LIBRARY ☙

To the right off the foyer is the library, which probably served as a gentlemen's retreat in the Whartons' day, a room of quiet but masculine elegance and one which featured several unusual and interesting decorative techniques. The wall treatment, original to Electra's occupancy of the house, is a fabric-backed covering with a special staining process

This large painted tapestry hung in the library in Mrs. Scott's day.

Stenciling in Library

ered with green varnish. The stenciling is in tones of blue, gold, tan and pink. Stenciling such as this, found throughout the house, is the only known stenciling on plaster extant in Fort Worth. The use of bronze such as the powder applied under the stenciling was common at the turn of the century to give the appearance of gold leaf or gilt at much less cost.

The leaded glass bookcases are of oak, rubbed when first cut with chromium oxide to give it a greenish cast. The millwork was probably done in St. Louis. These bookcases, like the woodwork, would have been highly polished. The library fireplace is of tile and probably held a metal gas-burning element.

Mrs. Scott had this room decorated much like the foyer in that it was filled with family memorabilia, framed photographs, and comfortable furniture. Because it was the library, the tabletop collections also included fine leather-bound books, small boxes, and small ceramic vases and porcelain pieces. Mrs. Scott loved porcelain and indulged in European buying sprees of Wedgewood, Limoges and other fine lines of china. Photographs show two rocking chairs, one of heavy wicker and the other of mahogany with a cane back, along with side chairs and an oval table. The

popular at the turn of the century. The wall was covered with a thin fabric to which a layer of heavy canvas wall covering was secured with a thick coat of animal-based glue. Aluminum leaf was then applied to the fabric and a green and amber varnish used to give an iridescent effect. Accented by antique-finished studs of either bronze or brass, this covering extends from the wainscoting to the picture rail. Above the picture rail, the plaster was decorated with elaborate stenciling completed over a bronze powder base cov-

The leaded glass bookcases in the library. Note the Tiffany lamp on the table.

The fireplace in the library.

contents were protected from the glaring Texas sun by roller shades, lace glass curtains and heavy draperies at the windows. Lighting in the library probably came from a brass chandelier and a pair of sconces mounted over the fireplace. A Tiffany-style lamp would have been placed on an occasional table.

T HE DRAWING ROOM ❧   Directly across from the library is the most formal room in the house, the parlor or drawing room. In the early part of this century in grand American homes, the drawing room was a place of stiff formality, with elegant, even delicate, furniture, and was used only on the most special occasions. The use of woods in the Thistle Hill drawing room varies from the rest of the downstairs, marking this as a more formal area. The floor is curly maple, and the fireplace trim and woodwork, mahogany. Although later painted, this mahogany would have been exposed in Electra's day.

The Rococo Revival style of the parlor today reflects Mrs. Scott's taste and the changes she made. The exposed woodwork has been painted, and plaster gar-

This view of a corner of the parlor and into the foyer was taken from the dining room.

The fireplace in the parlor or drawing room.

49

A corner of the parlor or drawing room.

A view from the parlor, across a corner of the dining room, and into the solarium at the side of the dining room.

lands, creating panels, were applied to the walls. It was widely held that these panels were without doubt gold leaf or gilt and that the room was appropriately called "The Gold Room," but chemical paint analysis during restoration uncovered no evidence of gold leaf in the room. Although Electra and A. B. had the room painted green and accented by the highly polished exposed wood, Mrs. Scott used a softer palette of grey for the mantel and walls and mauve for the panels within the garlands, with a highly stylized floral and ribbon motif stenciled on the plaster cove.

Draperies in this elegant room would have been fine brocade, probably with gilt cornices of the French style. As in the library, lace glass curtains and roller shades also would have been used. In contrast to the foyer, the drawing room would have been sparsely furnished but with elegant, formal furniture—gilt side chairs, a gilt marble-topped table, an elaborate wooden pedestal with a marble figure, probably a sofa. The room was less comfortable than elegant.

THE DINING ROOM ♣   The dining room
sits directly behind the drawing room. During the residence of both the Whartons and Mrs. Scott, this room was the scene of much elegant entertaining.

Originally, the room had wainscoting similar to that of the foyer. Photographs indicate it was intact after Mrs. Scott's 1912 remodeling, and it was probably removed only after her death, perhaps by the Girls Service League. The wall treatment was also similar to the foyer and the library, a fabric-backed, leather-like treatment unique to the period. In the late twenties or early thirties, the walls and ceiling were plastered with a heavily textured stucco, a decorating practice popular at that time.

Both the Whartons and Mrs. Scott would have used a large, round oak dining table in this room. The presence of such a table is supported by newspaper accounts of dinner parties given here, accounts which talk of as many as sixteen people seated at a large round table. Traditional furnishings in such a room would also have included a glass-sided china cabinet, probably angled into the corner between the doorways to the foyer and the drawing room, and a sideboard. Surfaces of the table and sideboard would have been covered with lace and protected with custom-cut glass. Finally, the room would probably have held two side chairs and almost certainly a tea cart.

The formal dining room, as Mrs. Scott decorated it, with the door to the morning room seen at the rear, left-hand corner of the picture.

A corner of the dining room, with the doors to the parlor pulled together.

53

THE SOLARIUM ♣

Originally, the solarium was a screened area adjacent to the dining room. Mrs. Scott enclosed it. Either way, it was created to be a cool, elegant addition to the dining area, and its classical simplicity, with marble wainscoting and scored plaster work, creates a light, dazzling effect. Marble was the focal point in this room, which probably held at least one large urn and a marble bench.

The fireplace in the dining room.

A view of the solarium, taken from the dining room.

THE MORNING ROOM ♣   Directly behind the dining room and solarium is the morning room, an addition to the original construction which was almost certainly made by the Scotts, probably during their 1912 remodeling. In the 1920s or early 1930s, Mrs. Scott remodeled the room again, principally because she wanted an exterior door leading to her formal gardens. At this time, she removed a built-in china cabinet and the wainscoting which matched the rest of the house, installing French doors, mirror-backed niches, and sconces not in keeping with the house itself. A stucco finish was applied to the plaster walls, but the tile and workmanship here are not similar to the rest of the house and clearly indicate a later date of remodeling. Sometime during its reign, the Girls Service League added a dropped acoustical ceiling and covered the strip oak floor with linoleum and carpet, so that by the 1980s when restoration plans were made, the morning room bore little resemblance to its original condition. The room has been partially restored to its 1912 look. The mirror-backed niches and stucco finish have been removed, revealing stenciling similar to that in other parts of the house.

The morning room.

THE KITCHEN ♣   The kitchen of the mansion retains several clues to the lives of past occupants. One of the most interesting is the annunciator board, a system by which the kitchen help could be summoned to various rooms in the house. Although not in working order, the board itself is still in the kitchen.

The kitchen has, of course, undergone several changes over the years, all aimed at increasing its functional usefulness rather than its historic quality. Its original condition is difficult to determine, but probably the exposed wood was highly polished, as in the rest of the house, and the floor may have been polished or painted wood or linoleum. The arched area on the south wall indicates the position of a wood-burning stove in the original kitchen.

In her remodeling, Mrs. Scott added the pantry in the southwest corner of the kitchen and enclosed the service porch on the west. The floor of this porch, tile leaded with black slate, matches the floor on the front porch of the house and is slanted to provide drainage, probably for wooden ice boxes.

THE GAME OR MUSIC ROOM ♣   The room opposite the dining room on the first floor has caused more controversy than any other area in the house. It has the same high wainscoting found throughout the downstairs, but the plate rail at the top of the wainscot is much larger. The panelling is fumed oak, a technique used to achieve a grainy, dark effect, and the fireplace, originally red brick though painted over several times, is massive, like a hunting lodge.

In the early years of the restoration effort, this room was called the Music Room, but it is architecturally not suited to be a music room. The deeply coffered ceiling would have trapped the sound, as would the wainscot and wide plate rail. Too, the wide expanse of windows makes it acoustically undesirable. Finally, the room has a rugged, masculine feel to it that clearly is not appropriate to a music room.

Several clues, from the massive fireplace to the wide plate rail suitable for trophies, suggest that this was instead a billiard room, and contemporary newspaper accounts verify this, referring to gaming and card parties in the room. Above the trophy rail and below the ceiling molding, the plaster has been treated in a deco-

57

Rubusmont

58

rative manner. Apparently pigment was mixed with glue and applied to wet plaster. Words and scrolls, possibly stenciled, are also evident near the top of the walls.

Etched into a plaque over the fireplace is the word "Rubusmont," a French or Latin term meaning "Thorn Mountain." It was Electra's name for her home; Mrs. Scott, in her determined effort to stamp her own identity on the house, had the name covered with a tapestry.

An outline left in the ceiling suggests that the original light fixture in this room was the type that hung above a billiard table in post-Victorian homes. It may well have had a gas jet for lighting gentlemen's cigars.

Although Mrs. Scott may have later used the room for music, it probably originally held a billiard table and cue case. There might have been sofas on either side of the fireplace, and comfortable arm chairs, convenient smoking stands, perhaps oak side chairs, and a gaming table.

The door in this room is of particular interest. It is a huge sliding door with a conventional door set into it. The inside is a single panel, but there are four panels on the exterior or foyer side, to match the other sliding doors opening onto the foyer. Nonetheless, the door is of one piece of wood. All other rooms downstairs have double sliding doors.

THE STAIRCASE ♣

Thistle Hill is built around a dramatic horseshoe staircase. The wide lower portion of the staircase, with its hand-turned balustrade, leads to a landing dominated by a Palladian window, its center portion crowned by a shell motif and flanked by two Tiffany-style windows, one inside the house and one outside. The one inside faces the servants' stairs from the kitchen to the second floor and the one outside overlooks the now-enclosed service porch.

Underneath the stairs on one side is the butler's pantry and on the other, the only downstairs lavatory, with the period marble fixtures intact.

The staircase breaks at the landing into two narrow sets of stairs leading to the open second floor hall. This hall is almost definitely changed in configuration from the original shape. To the right at the top of the stairs, a door has been added, creating a square corner which does not balance with the curve of the wall on the opposite side. The architect's original plan no doubt called for a symmetrical balance.

This hall, the most public space on the second floor, would have been elegantly furnished, with several comfortable places for sitting, mirrors to check one's

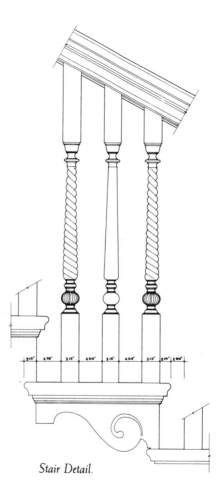

Stair Detail.

Detail at Stair Landing.

Column Detail.

appearance, and so on. Although the earliest wall finish here was dark green, with stenciling in the plaster coves, it was later covered with a fabric-backed wallcover. The original stenciling was a large, two-color design typical of the post-Victorian period.

THE MASTER BEDROOM, BATH AND DRESSING ROOM ♣

The master bedroom is to the east of the stairs, a large, sunny room which Mrs. Scott undoubtedly used as a combination bedroom and sitting room. Probably the decoration of the room reflected her fondness for French taste—a French style chandelier and sconces, delicate Louis XV furniture, a gilt wall mirror. Here the carpet would most likely have been a Brussels or Wilton in pastel shades, probably with a small floral motif. Family photos and mementos probably sat on the tables or lady's writing desk in this room, but there would have been no pictures or paintings on the walls. Mrs. Scott's decor for the bedroom apparently relied heavily on the then-popular book, *The House of Good Taste*, by Elsie deWolfe. According to deWolfe, it would have been in poor taste to decorate the walls in a bedroom. She also advised heavy use of chintz and declared armoires hopelessly out of date. Thistle Hill had no armoires during either Electra or Elizabeth's occupancy.

The closet in the master bedroom has a small wall safe. It was here that Electra looked frantically for jewelry she thought A.B. had hidden from her to teach her the importance of locking up her valuables. The safe was empty, and Electra's jewelry is presumed to have been stolen, for it was never found.

The bathroom adjacent to the master bedroom was changed dramatically during the 1912 remodeling. The original fixtures were replaced, no doubt in response to city requirements. The original bathtubs throughout the house filled from a faucet near the bottom of the tub, instead of filling from the top as do bathtubs today, but a city ordinance banned the use of such tubs because of their tendency to back up. This bathroom is rumored to have had the first bidet in Fort Worth.

Although there is no fireplace in the master bedroom, there is one in what was probably Mrs. Scott's personal dressing room. Wealthy women in that period were advised to divide large bedroom areas into several smaller rooms: antechamber, sleeping room, dressing room, sitting room. The use of this room as a dressing room is confirmed by the presence of the

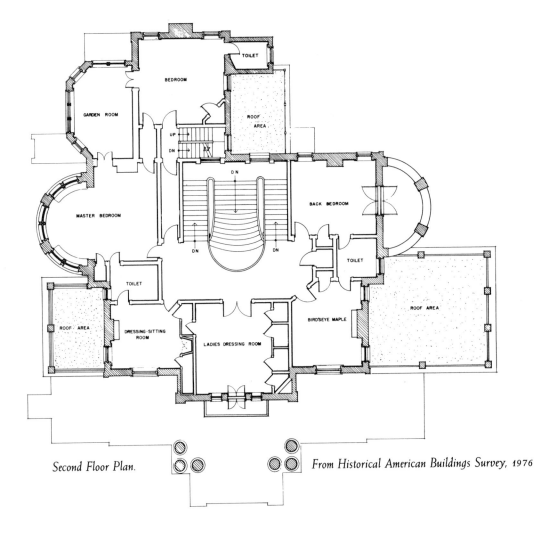

62

Second Floor Plan.   *From Historical American Buildings Survey, 1976*

three-cornered mirror and the fireplace. Ladies were encouraged to indulge in the luxury of making one's toilet before an open fire, especially if they had, for health's sake, slept in the chill air provided by open windows.

THE SLEEPING PORCH ♣

The sleeping porch is on the other side of the master bedroom from the bath, above the morning room. This, too, was added by Mrs. Scott. Sleeping porches were not common in elegant homes of the period but are perfectly suited to Mrs. Scott's West Texas background. And this room is ideally located to catch any breezes. A circular porcelain grill in the ceiling allowed circulation from a wind turbine.

The porch was probably casually furnished, suited to its nature. There may have been a white painted iron bedstead, a straw mat on the floor, perhaps a wicker table or tea cart, and wicker sofa and armchairs, with cushions of bright fabric (perhaps chintz which was extremely fashionable in wealthy homes of the period).

THE BOYS' ROOM OR NURSERY ♣

This room, originally connected to the master bedroom by a short hall, has light on three sides and is one of the airiest rooms in the house. Although it is sometimes called the nursery, Mrs. Scott's son was well past nursery age when he occupied it. The bathroom adjacent to this room is over the pantry and like it was added by Mrs. Scott.

The boys' room was probably furnished with rather plain, serviceable pieces, mostly painted white—an iron bedstead, a pair of night stands, one or two chests of drawers, a table or a student's desk.

The boys room also opens into a short hall providing access to the servants' stairs from kitchen to third floor. These stairs are of pine, the only pine flooring used in the entire house. One Tiffany-style window from the landing of the main staircase looms above them.

THE BIRD'S-EYE MAPLE ROOM ♣

This guest room is unique because of the consistent use of bird's-eye maple, in contrast to the wood of the other

Fireplace Elevation–Bird's-Eye Maple Room

rooms. The use of this wood on the fireplace is particularly dramatic, and while even the doors of the room are maple, their exterior surfaces are veneer to match other doors opening into public areas of the house.

The furniture in this room was also no doubt maple—a bedstead, night stand, bureau, skirted dressing table. Chintz was probably used in the dust ruffle on the bed, the skirt on the dressing table, even the upholstery of a large and comfortable chair. Although a large maple armoire stood in this room for several years, it would not have been part of either Mrs. Wharton's or Mrs. Scott's decorating scheme.

The maple room and the other second floor guest room are connected by a bathroom which still has its original fixtures, including a lighting fixture designed to accommodate either gas or electricity and a marble lavatory and footed tub thought to date to 1903.

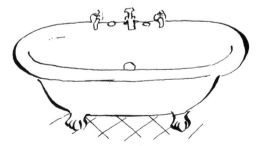

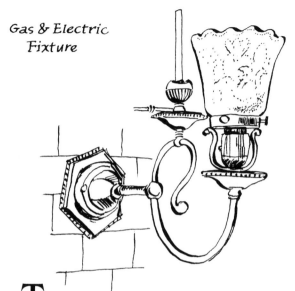

THE MAHOGANY GUEST ROOM ♣ The second or rear guest room in the house is all mahogany, more in keeping perhaps with the general tone of the house. In this room, one can particularly notice the bead and reel work (a tiny beaded cord) along the woodwork. Though it is used throughout the house, this detail shows up best in this guest room.

This room probably once had floral and striped wallpaper and was furnished with either oak or mahogany pieces.

Casement doors open from this room directly onto a semicircular porch.

THE UPSTAIRS SITTING ROOM ♣ In the early years of the house, this room, in the center of the upstairs hall, was probably both a dressing room and sitting room, an area where ladies could retire to refresh themselves after a long journey, particularly in the early automobiles. Automobile travel in that day was tiresome and dusty, to say the least.

Mrs. Scott installed the wall of closets, making the room more definitively a dressing room for guests, and in so doing covered up a fireplace. She probably had the room furnished with a dressing table which held assorted bottles and jars of makeup, a washstand with bowl and pitcher, since the room is not adjacent to a bathroom, and several comfortable chairs or a sofa. In keeping with her taste, there was no doubt a round oak table covered with family memorabilia.

65

THE THIRD FLOOR ♣   Like the game/ music room, the third floor of Thistle Hill has caused some controversy, revolving around the large room that may or may not have been a ballroom. The third floor is reached by the servants' stairs, off the small hallway which is adjacent to the master bedroom and leads to the boys' room. It is an awkward location for stairs to a grand ballroom, but the stairs, now enclosed to meet fire code requirements, were once open, making them a little more accessible. A similar house in Dallas, the Munger residence, also designed by Sanguinet, had a third-floor room finished in much the same way, and it was known to be used for parties. A niece of Electra Wharton's, Mrs. Electra Waggoner Biggs, reported that her mother talked of attending parties in the ballroom at Thistle Hill.

Newspaper accounts of the Whartons' parties also support the notion that this was a party room, although in all probability, the Whartons never used it as a grand ballroom. Mrs. Scott probably did not entertain there.

The so-called ballroom is a large room with diagonal flooring, tongue and groove walls, and sloping ceiling, also tongue and groove. The former dormer windows, covered by Mrs. Scott, can be seen in this room.

The third floor also has two servants' rooms, one with the original and probably now-valuable straw matting on the floor, and one with a full bath. One of the servants rooms has a Palladian window so that the exterior appearance complements the overall style of the house.

THE BASEMENT ♣   The basement at Thistle Hill contains a large laundry room, a wine or pantry storage, a servants' bathroom, a furnace room, and a coal storage bin. The house was built with a hot water or low pressure steam boiler heating system which was originally coal-burning but was converted to gas in the 1940s. The original radiators may still be seen throughout the house.

The Restoration

TEN YEARS AFTER the house was purchased, it still looked the same. A restoration expert might have noticed that the roof had been repaired and the most badly deteriorated windows replaced, but these repairs were not obvious to the casual observer. Nor was the rewiring inside, a process which further damaged and scarred interior walls rather than improving the appearance of the house but did bring the building up to the fire safety code. The grand staircase had been restored, and though it didn't look much different, it was once again safe to climb. Outside, the exterior buildings—the carriage house, the pergola and the tea house—had been restored. But inside the ceilings showed cracks, the walls in the parlor and library were streaked and dirty, the furniture in the house was scanty and sometimes inappropriate to the period.

Restoration necessarily begins behind the scenes. The unglamorous structural work—roof repair to prevent water damage, foundation repair to keep the house from shifting and buckling, wiring and plumbing repair to ensure safety from fire or burst pipes—is necessary if the cosmetic work, the restoration decoration, is to survive. Restoration also always begins from the top, hence the initial attention to the roof and windows. This order of progression insures the permanence of work undertaken. Even in the final decorating of a restored room, work proceeds from ceiling to floor, so that work on the ceiling does not damage or mar previously done floor work.

For a decade, restoration progressed at an even pace at Thistle Hill even though much of it was not readily apparent. The first step in any major project is a Historic American Building Survey which presents measured drawings or architectural elevations, cross-sectional drawings, and drawings of such major details as fireplaces, windows, doors and staircases. It provides a starting point for the long process. At Thistle Hill, this survey was done in the mid-1970s by architectural students from the University of Texas at Arlington.

The next step is a historic structures report, usually done by an architect or architectural consultant who is considered an expert on historic structures. This report documents the evolution of the house, tracing the changes made by individual occupants, and provides a basis for determining the direction of restoration. Kathryn Livingston, now certified by the American Institute of Architecture (AIA), prepared the Thistle Hill report in 1980. Her report demonstrated the impracticality of restoring Thistle Hill to its original 1903 condition, documenting irreversible changes made by the 1912 remodeling. Livingston recommended the goal adopted by Texas Heritage—restoring the house to its 1912 appearance.

In 1982, the Austin architectural firm of Bell, Klein and Hoffman drew up a master plan. This plan, the next step after the historic structures report, provided a road map for the restoration process, suggesting the order of steps to be taken and even estimating costs.

Paint and wall covering analysis was done in 1984 by Frank Welch, a chemist who is a historic paint consultant. By taking samples from the walls at various points, Welch was able to identify the nature of the wall covering, materials used and method of application. It was, for example, his analysis which uncovered the unusual wall treatment in the library. This study included both interior and exterior paint, wood stain throughout the house, and exterior mortar.

The furnishing plan for the mansion was done by Michael Berry, curator of interiors for the National Trust for Historic Preservation. Berry's report, a room-by-room description, suggests furnishings that would duplicate or resemble those ordered by Mrs. Scott. Relying heavily on available photographs, Berry rec-

ommended, for instance, the heavy use of bric-a-brac throughout the downstairs rooms.

The steps of the restoration process build one upon the other. The historic building survey provides a background for the historic structures report which, in turn, provides a background for the master plan. During this building process, information may often be contradicted by new discoveries.

For example, the historic structures report dates the upstairs bathroom, off the master bedroom, as a product of the 1912 remodeling, but paint analysis has clearly linked that room to the paint in areas original to the house. The logical then becomes obvious: Would a pampered woman like Electra Waggoner Wharton have lived with a bathroom clear across the upstairs landing? Restoration teaches one never to assume earlier information is correct.

Restoration at Thistle Hill is not complete, and no target date can be suggested for completion. Cosmetic repair took a giant step forward when Texas Heritage, Inc., joined with the Historic Preservation Council for Tarrant County to make the home the 1987 Designers Showhouse, reversing the refusal years earlier of the Save-the-Scott group to allow such use of the home.

Whereas earlier it was feared that the designers might blur the restoration process, in 1987 the approach was one of restorative treatment. The designers, who viewed the showhouse as a community service project, agreed not to compromise wall treatments—no nail holes, no paint on exposed woodwork. The showhouse was a triumph for both its designers and Thistle Hill, bringing several thousand people into the house which, for the first time since its public opening, looked more like the grand home it once was, less a shabby shadow of its former self.

But restoration is a never-ending process, and few projects are ever complete. Every time a wall is opened for repairs or a floor pulled up for plumbing work, new information is uncovered. The scope and philosophy of the project can change, in response to new information, at every step of the process.

Thistle Hill may not have been complete ten years after its purchase for restoration, and it may not ever be finished, but it is an essential part of the historic community in Fort Worth. Operated by Texas Heritage, Inc., the mansion is used for weddings and spook houses, special Christmas events and old-time festivals which recapture the days of its glory. Daily tours are given by docents, and it has even been used as the setting for a television show. The standards set when the house was first purchased remain firm today: no events are allowed which might in any way damage or permanently change the interior or exterior of the building.

Thistle Hill is important to Fort Worth because so many of the city's people attend various functions there. But its importance goes beyond that of a social center. The mansion stands as a landmark, a visible reminder of the city's cattle baron legacy. And in a city that takes its history seriously, the restoration of Thistle Hill provides encouragement and inspiration for the restoration of other historic sites. Fort Worth now boasts individual structures and several multi-block areas which have been either restored or renovated. It all began with a group of determined citizens who believed that saving a historic home was important and who proved that it was possible. It all began with Thistle Hill.

Thistle Hill

Text set in Weiss with Benguiat titles
by G&S Typesetters, Austin
Printed and bound by Braun-Brumfield, Ann Arbor
Designed and produced by
Whitehead & Whitehead, Austin
1988